Billy is hiding

Story by Annette Smith
Illustrations by Betty Greenhatch

Mom said,

"Come here, Jack.

Come here, Billy."

Jack ran to Mom.

"We are going in the car,"
said Mom.
"Where is Billy?"

"Where are you, Billy?"

said Jack.

"Come here, Billy," said Mom.

"We are going in the car."

Mom and Jack
looked and looked
for Billy.

"Billy is hiding," said Mom.

"I can not see Billy," said Mom.

"He is not in here,"

said Jack.

Mom looked in the box.

Jack looked on the big chair.

"Look, Mom!" said Jack.

"Come on, Jack," said Mom.
"Billy is not here."

"Boo!" said Billy.

"Here I am!"